&s OLD &s CHRISTMAS

FROM THE SKETCH BOOK OF
WASHINGTON IRVING

ILLUSTRATED BY
RANDOLPH CALDECOTT

APPLEWOOD BOOKS
Bedford, Massachusetts

Old Christmas
was originally published in
1886

ISBN: 978-1-4290-1668-1

For a free copy of our current print catalog featuring our bestselling books, write to:

APPLEWOOD BOOKS
P.O. Box 365
Bedford, MA 01730

For more complete listings, visit us on the web at:
awb.com

Prepared for publishing by HP

CHRISTMAS

"The old family mansion, partly thrown in deep shadow, and partly lit up by the cold moonshine
—*Frontispiece*.

OLD CHRISTMAS.

FROM THE
Sketch of Book
Washington Irving.

ILLUSTRATED BY R. CALDECOTT

London.
Macmillan & Co

1886

But is old, old, good old Christmas gone?
Nothing but the hair of his good, gray, old
head and beard left? Well, I will have that,
seeing that I cannot have more of him.

Hue and Cry after Christmas.

BEFORE the remembrance of the good old times, so fast passing, should have entirely passed away, the present artist, R. Caldecott, and engraver, James D. Cooper, planned to illustrate Washington Irving's "Old Christmas" in this manner. Their primary idea was to carry out the principle of the Sketch Book, by incorporating the designs with the text. Throughout they have worked together and *con amore*. With what success the public must decide.

NOVEMBER 1875.

CONTENTS

LIST OF ILLUSTRATIONS

DESIGNED BY RANDOLPH CALDECOTT,

AND

ARRANGED AND ENGRAVED BY J. D. COOPER.

CHRISTMAS

A man might then behold
    At Christmas, in each hall
Good fires to curb the cold,
    And meat for great and small.
The neighbours were friendly bidden,
    And all had welcome true,
The poor from the gates were not chidden,
    When this old cap was new.

Old Song.

THERE is nothing in England that exercises a more delightful spell over my imagination than the lingerings of the holiday customs and rural games of former times. They recall the pictures my fancy used to draw in the May morning of life, when as yet I only knew the world through books, and believed it to be all that poets had painted it; and they bring with them the flavour of those honest days of yore, in which, perhaps with equal fallacy, I am apt to think the world was more home-bred, social, and joyous than at present. I regret to say that they are daily growing more and more faint, being gradually

worn away by time, but still more obliterated by
modern fashion. They resemble those picturesque morsels of Gothic architecture which we

see crumbling in various parts of the country,
partly dilapidated by the waste of ages, and partly
lost in the additions and alterations of latter days.
Poetry, however, clings with cherishing fondness
about the rural game and holiday revel, from

which it has derived so many of its themes—as
the ivy winds its rich foliage about the Gothic
arch and mouldering tower, gratefully repaying
their support by clasping together their tottering
remains, and, as it were, embalming them in
verdure.

Of all the old festivals, however, that of
Christmas awakens the strongest and most heartfelt associations. There is a tone of solemn and
sacred feeling that blends with our conviviality,
and lifts the spirit to a state of hallowed and
elevated enjoyment. The services of the church
about this season are extremely tender and inspiring. They dwell on the beautiful story of the
origin of our faith, and the pastoral scenes that
accompanied its announcement. They gradually
increase in fervour and pathos during the season
of Advent, until they break forth in full jubilee on
the morning that brought peace and good-will
to men. I do not know a grander effect of
music on the moral feelings than to hear the

full choir and the pealing organ performing a Christmas anthem in a cathedral, and filling every part of the vast pile with triumphant harmony.

It is a beautiful arrangement, also, derived from days of yore, that this festival, which commemorates the announcement of the religion of peace and love, has been made the season for gathering together of family

connections, and drawing closer again those bands
of kindred hearts which the cares and pleasures
and sorrows of the world are continually operating
to cast loose;
of calling back
the children of
a family who
have launched
forth in life,
and wandered
widely asunder,
once more to
assemble about
the paternal hearth,
that rallying-place of the affections, there to grow
young and loving again among the endearing
mementoes of childhood.

There is something in the very season of the
year that gives a charm to the festivity of Christmas. At other times we derive a great portion
of our pleasures from the mere beauties of nature.

Our feelings sally forth and dissipate themselves
over the sunny landscape, and we "live abroad
and everywhere." The song of the bird, the
murmur of the stream, the breathing fragrance
of spring, the soft voluptuousness of summer, the
golden pomp of autumn; earth with its mantle
of refreshing green, and heaven with its deep
delicious blue and its cloudy magnificence, all fill
us with mute but exquisite delight, and we revel
in the luxury of mere sensation. But in the
depth of winter, when nature lies despoiled of
every charm, and wrapped in her shroud of

sheeted snow, we turn for our gratifications to
moral sources. The dreariness and desolation
of the landscape, the short gloomy days and

darksome nights, while they circumscribe our wanderings, shut in our feelings also from rambling abroad, and make us more keenly disposed for the pleasures of the social circle. Our thoughts are more concentrated; our friendly sympathies more aroused. We feel more sensibly the charm of each other's society, and are brought more closely together by dependence on each other for enjoyment. Heart calleth unto heart; and we draw our pleasures from the deep wells of living kindness, which lie in the quiet recesses of our bosoms; and which, when resorted to, furnish forth the pure element of domestic felicity.

The pitchy gloom without makes the heart dilate on entering the room filled with the glow and warmth of the evening fire. The ruddy blaze diffuses an artificial summer and sunshine through the room, and lights up each countenance into a kindlier welcome. Where does the honest face of hospitality expand into a broader

and more cordial smile—where is the shy glance
of love more sweetly eloquent—than by the

winter fireside ? and as the hollow blast of wintry
wind rushes through the hall, claps the distant

door, whistles about the casement, and rumbles
down the chimney, what can be more grateful
than that feeling of sober and sheltered security
with which we look round upon the comfortable
chamber and the scene of domestic hilarity ?

The English, from the great prevalence of
rural habits throughout every class of society,
have always been fond of those festivals and
holidays which agreeably interrupt the stillness
of country life ; and they were, in former days,
particularly observant of the religious and social
rites of Christmas. It is inspiring to read even
the dry details which some antiquarians have
given of the quaint humours, the burlesque
pageants, the complete abandonment to mirth
and good-fellowship, with which this festival was
celebrated. It seemed to throw open every door,
and unlock every heart. It brought the peasant
and the peer together, and blended all ranks in
one warm generous flow of joy and kindness.
The old halls of castles and manor-houses re-

sounded with the harp and the Christmas carol, and their ample boards groaned under the weight of hospitality. Even the poorest cottage welcomed the festive sea-son with green decorations of bay and holly—the cheerful fire glanced its rays through the lattice, inviting the pass-enger to raise the latch, and join the gossip knot huddled round the hearth, beguiling the long evening with le-gendary jokes and oft-told Christmas tales.

One of the least pleasing effects of modern refinement is the havoc it has made among the hearty old holiday customs. It has completely taken off the sharp touchings and spirited reliefs of these embellishments of life, and has worn down society into a more smooth and polished,

but certainly a less characteristic surface.   Many
of the games and ceremonials of Christmas have
entirely disappeared, and, like the sherris sack
of old Falstaff, are become matters of speculation and dispute among commentators.   They
flourished in times full of spirit and lustihood,
when men enjoyed life roughly, but heartily and
vigorously ; times wild and picturesque, which
have furnished poetry with its richest materials,
and the drama with its most attractive variety of
characters and manners.   The world has become
more worldly.   There is more of dissipation, and
less of enjoyment.   Pleasure has expanded into
a broader, but a shallower stream, and has for-
saken many of those deep and quiet channels
where it flowed sweetly through the calm bosom
of domestic life.   Society has acquired a more
enlightened and elegant tone ; but it has lost
many of its strong local peculiarities, its home-
bred feelings, its honest fireside delights.   The
traditionary customs of golden-hearted antiquity,

its feudal hospitalities, and lordly wassailings,
have passed away with the baronial castles and
stately manor-houses in which they were cele-

brated. They comported with the shadowy
hall, the great oaken gallery, and the tapes-
tried parlour, but are unfitted to the light showy

saloons and gay drawing-rooms of the modern
villa.

Shorn, however, as it is, of its ancient and
festive honours, Christmas is still a period of
delightful excitement in England. It is gratify-
ing to see that home-feeling completely aroused
which seems to hold so powerful a place in every
English bosom. The preparations making on
every side for the social board that is again to
unite friends and kindred ; the presents of good
cheer passing and repassing, those tokens of
regard, and quickeners of kind feelings ; the ever-
greens distributed about houses and churches,
emblems of peace and gladness ; all these have
the most pleasing effect in producing fond associations, and kindling benevolent sympathies. Even
the sound of the waits, rude as may be their
minstrelsy, breaks upon the mid-watches of a
winter night with the effect of perfect harmony.
As I have been awakened by them in that still
and solemn hour, " when deep sleep falleth upon

man," I have listened with a hushed delight, and connecting them with the sacred and joyous occasion, have almost fancied them into another celestial choir, announcing peace and good-will to mankind.

How delightfully the imagination, when wrought upon by these moral influences, turns everything to melody and beauty : The very crowing of the cock, who is sometimes heard in the profound repose of the country, "telling the night watches to his feathery dames," was thought by the common people to announce the approach of this sacred festival :—

" Some say that ever 'gainst that season comes
  Wherein our Saviour's birth is celebrated,
  This bird of dawning singeth all night long :
  And then, they say, no spirit dares stir abroad ;
  The nights are wholesome—then no planets strike,
  No fairy takes, no witch hath power to charm,
  So hallow'd and so gracious is the time."

Amidst the general call to happiness, the bustle of the spirits, and stir of the affections, which prevail at this period, what bosom can remain insensible ? It is, indeed, the season of re-generated feeling—the season for kindling, not merely the fire of hospitality in the hall, but the genial flame of charity in the heart.

The scene of early love again rises green to memory beyond the sterile waste of years ; and the idea of home, fraught with the fragrance of home-dwelling joys, re-animates the drooping spirit,—as the Arabian breeze will sometimes waft the freshness of the distant fields to the weary pilgrim of the desert.

Stranger and sojourner as I am in the land —though for me no social hearth may blaze, no hospitable roof throw open its doors, nor the warm grasp of friendship welcome me at the threshold—yet I feel the influence of the season beaming into my soul from the happy looks of those around me.   Surely happiness is reflective, like the light of heaven ; and every countenance, bright with smiles, and glowing with innocent enjoyment, is a mirror transmitting to others the

rays of a supreme and ever-shining benevolence. He who can turn churlishly away from contemplating the felicity of his fellow-beings, and sit down darkling and repining in his loneliness when all around is joyful, may have his moments of strong excitement and selfish gratification, but he wants the genial and social sympathies which constitute the charm of a merry Christmas.

The Stage Coach

Omne benè
Sine pœnâ
Tempus est ludendi ;
Venit hora,
Absque morâ,
Libros deponendi.

Old Holiday School Song.

THE STAGE COACH

N the preceding paper I have made some general observations on the Christmas festivities of England, and am tempted to illustrate them by some anecdotes of a Christmas passed in the country; in perusing which I would most courteously invite my reader to lay aside the austerity of wisdom, and to put on that genuine holiday spirit which is tolerant of folly, and anxious only for amusement.

In the course of a December tour in Yorkshire, I rode for a long distance in one of the public coaches, on the day preceding Christmas.

The coach was crowded, both inside and out, with passengers, who, by their talk, seemed principally bound to the mansions of relations or friends to eat the Christmas dinner. It was loaded also with hampers of game, and baskets and boxes of delicacies; and hares hung dangling their long ears about the coachman's box,—presents from

 distant friends for the impending feast. I had three fine rosy-cheeked schoolboys for my fellow-passengers inside, full of the buxom health and

manly spirit which I have observed in the children of this country. They were returning home for the holidays in high glee, and promising themselves a world of enjoyment. It was delightful to hear the gigantic plans of pleasure of the little rogues, and the impracticable feats they were to perform during their six weeks' emancipation from the abhorred thraldom of book, birch, and pedagogue. They were full of anticipations of the meeting with the family and household, down to the very cat and dog; and of the joy they were to give their little sisters by the presents with which their pockets were crammed; but the meeting to which they seemed to look forward with the greatest impatience was with Bantam, which I found to be a pony, and, according to their talk, possessed of more virtues than any steed since the days of Bucephalus. How he could trot! how he could run! and then such leaps as he would take—there was not a hedge in the whole country that he could not clear.

They were under the particular guardianship of the coachman, to whom, whenever an oppor- tunity presented, they addressed a host of ques- tions, and pronounced him one of the best fellows in the whole world. Indeed, I could not but notice the more than ordinary air of bustle and

importance of the coachman, who wore his hat a
little on one side, and had a large bunch of Christmas greens stuck in the button-hole of his coat.
He is always a personage full of mighty care
and business, but he is particularly so during this
season, having so many commissions to execute in
consequence of the great interchange of presents.
And here, perhaps, it may not be unacceptable
to my untravelled readers, to have a sketch that
may serve as a general representation of
this very numerous and important class of
functionaries, who have a dress, a manner, a
language, an air, peculiar to themselves, and
prevalent throughout the fraternity; so that,
wherever an English stage-coachman may be
seen, he cannot be mistaken for one of any other
craft or mystery.

He has commonly a broad, full face, curiously
mottled with red, as if the blood had been forced
by hard feeding into every vessel of the skin; he
is swelled into jolly dimensions by frequent pota-

tions of malt liquors, and his bulk is still fur-
ther increased by a multiplicity of coats, in
which he is buried like a cauliflower, the upper

one reaching to his heels.   He wears a broad-
brimmed, low-crowned hat ; a huge roll of coloured
handkerchief about his neck, knowingly knotted

and tucked in at the bosom; and has in summer - time a large bouquet of flowers in his
button-hole; the present, most probably, of some
enamoured country lass. His waistcoat is commonly of some bright colour, striped; and his
small-clothes extend far below the knees, to meet
a pair of jockey boots which reach about half-way
up his legs.

All this costume is maintained with much pre-
cision; he has a pride in having his clothes of
excellent materials; and, notwithstanding the
seeming grossness of his appearance, there is still
discernible that neatness and propriety of person,
which is almost inherent in an Englishman. He
enjoys great consequence and consideration along
the road; has frequent conferences with the village housewives, who look upon him as a man of
great trust and dependence; and he seems to
have a good understanding with every bright-
eyed country lass. The moment he arrives where
the horses are to be changed, he throws down the

reins with something of an air, and abandons the
cattle to the care of the ostler; his duty being

merely to drive from one stage to another.
When off the box, his hands are thrust in the
pockets of his greatcoat, and he rolls about the
inn-yard with an air of the most absolute lordli-

ness.   Here he is generally surrounded by an
admiring throng of ostlers, stable-boys, shoe-blacks,

and those nameless hangers-on that infest inns
and taverns, and run errands, and do all kinds of

odd jobs, for the privilege of battening on the drippings of the kitchen and the leakage of the tap-room. These all look up to him as to an oracle; treasure up his cant phrases; echo his opinions about horses and other topics of jockey lore ; and, above all, endeavour to imitate his air and carriage. Every ragamuffin that has a coat to his back thrusts his hands in the pockets, rolls in his gait, talks slang, and is an embryo Coachey.

Perhaps it might be owing to the pleasing serenity that reigned in my own mind, that I fancied I saw cheerfulness in every countenance throughout the journey. A stage coach, however, carries animation always with it, and puts the world in motion as it whirls along. The horn sounded at the entrance of a village, produces a general bustle. Some hasten forth to meet friends; some with bundles and bandboxes to secure places, and in the hurry of the moment can hardly take leave of the group that accompanies

them. In the meantime, the coachman has a
world of small commissions to execute. Sometimes he delivers a hare or pheasant; sometimes
jerks a small parcel or newspaper to the door of a

public-house; and sometimes, with knowing leer
and words of sly import, hands to some half-
blushing, half-laughing housemaid an odd-shaped

billet-doux from some rustic admirer. As the
coach rattles through the village, every one runs
to the window, and you have glances on every
side of fresh country faces, and blooming giggling
girls. At the corners are assembled juntas of
village idlers and wise men, who take their sta-
tions there for the important purpose of seeing
company pass; but the sagest knot is generally
at the blacksmith's, to whom the passing of the
coach is an event fruitful of much speculation.

The smith, with the horse's heel in his lap, pauses
as the vehicle whirls by; the Cyclops round the
anvil suspend their ringing hammers, and suffer
the iron to grow cool; and the sooty spectre in
brown paper cap, labouring at the bellows, leans
on the handle for a moment, and permits the

asthmatic engine to heave a long-drawn sigh, while he glares through the murky smoke and sulphureous gleams of the smithy.

Perhaps the impending holiday might have given a more than usual animation to the country, for it seemed to me as if everybody was in good looks and good spirits. Game, poultry, and other luxuries of the table, were in brisk circulation in the villages; the grocers', butchers', and fruiterers' shops were thronged with customers. The housewives were stirring briskly about, putting their dwellings in order; and the glossy branches of holly, with their bright red berries, began to appear at the windows. The scene brought to mind an old writer's account of Christmas preparations:—" Now capons and hens, besides turkeys, geese, and ducks, with beef and mutton—must all die; for in twelve days a multitude of people will not be fed with a little. Now plums and spice, sugar and honey, square it among pies and broth. Now or never must

music be in tune, for the youth must dance and sing to get them a heat, while the aged sit by the fire. The country maid leaves half

her market, and must be sent again, if she forgets a pack of cards on Christmas eve. Great is the contention of Holly and Ivy, whether master or dame wears the breeches. Dice and cards benefit the butler; and if the cook do not lack wit, he will sweetly lick his fingers."

I was roused from this fit of luxurious meditation by a shout from my little travelling companions. They had been looking out of the coach-windows for the last few miles, recognising every tree and cottage as they approached home, and now there was a general burst of joy— "There's John! and there's old Carlo! and there's Bantam!" cried the happy little rogues, clapping their hands.

At the end of a lane there was an old sober-looking servant in livery waiting for them: he was accompanied by a superannuated pointer, and by the redoubtable Bantam, a little old rat of a pony, with a shaggy mane and long rusty tail, who stood dozing quietly by the roadside,

D

little dreaming of the bustling times that awaited him.

I was pleased to see the fondness with which the little fellows leaped about the steady old footman, and hugged the pointer, who wriggled his whole body for joy. But Bantam was the great object of interest; all wanted to mount at once; and it was with some difficulty that John arranged that they should ride by turns, and the eldest should ride first.

Off they set at last; one on the pony, with the dog bounding and barking before him, and the others holding John's hands ; both talking at once, and overpowering him by questions about home, and with school anecdotes. I looked after them with a feeling in which I do not know whether pleasure or melancholy predominated : for I was reminded of those days when, like them, I had neither known care nor sorrow, and a holiday was the summit of earthly felicity. We stopped a few moments afterwards to water the horses, and on resuming our route, a turn of the road brought us in sight of a neat country-seat. I could just distinguish the forms of a lady and

two young girls in the portico, and I saw my
little comrades, with Bantam, Carlo, and old John,
trooping along the carriage road. I leaned out
of the coach-window, in hopes of witnessing the
happy meeting, but a grove of trees shut it from
my sight.

In the evening we reached a village where I
had determined to pass the night. As we drove
into the great gateway of the inn, I saw on one
side the light of a rousing kitchen fire, beaming
through a window. I entered, and admired, for
the hundredth time, that picture of convenience,
neatness, and broad honest enjoyment, the kitchen of an English inn. It was of spacious
dimensions, hung round with copper and tin
vessels highly polished, and decorated here and
there with a Christmas green. Hams, tongues,
and flitches of bacon, were suspended from the
ceiling; a smoke-jack made its ceaseless clanking
beside the fireplace, and a clock ticked in one
corner. A well-scoured deal table extended along

one side of the kitchen, with a cold round of beef, and other hearty viands upon it, over which two

foaming tankards of ale seemed mounting guard. Travellers of inferior order were preparing to

attack this stout repast, while others sat smoking
and gossiping over their ale on two high-backed
oaken seats beside the fire. Trim housemaids
were hurrying backwards and forwards under the
directions of a fresh, bustling landlady; but still
seizing an occasional moment to exchange a
flippant word, and have a rallying laugh, with
the group round the fire. The scene completely
realised Poor Robin's humble idea of the comforts
of mid-winter.

> Now trees their leafy hats do bare,
> To reverence Winter's silver hair ;
> A handsome hostess, merry host,
> A pot of ale now and a toast,
> Tobacco and a good coal fire,
> Are things this season doth require.*

I had not been long at the inn when a post-
chaise drove up to the door. A young gentleman
stepped out, and by the light of the lamps I caught
a glimpse of a countenance which I thought I
knew. I moved forward to get a nearer view,

* Poor Robin's Almanack, 1684.

when his eye caught mine. I was not mistaken;
it was Frank Bracebridge, a sprightly good-
humoured young fellow, with whom I had once
travelled on the Continent. Our meeting was
extremely cordial; for the countenance of an old
fellow-traveller always brings up the recollection
of a thousand pleasant scenes, odd adventures,
and excellent jokes. To discuss all these in a
transient interview at an inn was impossible; and
finding that I was not pressed for time, and was
merely making a tour of observation, he insisted
that I should give him a day or two at his father's
country-seat, to which he was going to pass the
holidays, and which lay at a few miles' distance.
"It is better than eating a solitary Christmas
dinner at an inn," said he; "and I can assure
you of a hearty welcome in something of the
old-fashion style." His reasoning was cogent;
and I must confess the preparation I had seen for
universal festivity and social enjoyment had made
me feel a little impatient of my loneliness. I

closed, therefore, at once with his invitation : the chaise drove up to the door; and in a few moments I was on my way to the family mansion of the Bracebridges.

CHRISTMAS EVE

Saint Francis and Saint Benedight
Blesse this house from wicked wight ;
From the night-mare and the goblin,
That is hight good-fellow Robin ;
Keep it from all evil spirits,
Fairies, weezels, rats, and ferrets :
    From curfew time
    To the next prime.

                  CARTWRIGHT.

CHRISTMAS EVE

T was a brilliant moonlight night, but extremely cold; our chaise whirled rapidly over the frozen ground; the post-boy smacked his whip incessantly, and a part of the time his horses were on a gallop. "He knows where he is going," said my companion, laughing, "and is eager to arrive in time for some of the merriment and good cheer of the servants' hall. My father, you must know, is a bigoted devotee of the old school, and prides

himself upon keeping up something of old English
hospitality.   He is a tolerable specimen of what
you will rarely meet with now-a-days in its purity,
the old English country gentleman ; for our men
of fortune spend so much of their time in town,
and fashion is carried so much into the country,
that the strong rich peculiarities of ancient rural
life are almost polished away.   My father, however, from early years, took honest Peacham * for
his text book, instead of Chesterfield : he determined, in his own mind, that there was no condi-
tion more truly honourable and enviable than that
of a country gentleman on his paternal lands, and,
therefore, passes the whole of his time on his
estate.   He is a strenuous advocate for the revival
of the old rural games and holiday observances,
and is deeply read in the writers, ancient
and modern, who have treated on the subject.
Indeed, his favourite range of reading is among
the authors who flourished at least two centuries

* Peacham's Complete Gentleman, 1622.

since ; who, he insists, wrote and thought more like true Englishmen than any of their successors. He even regrets sometimes that he had not been born a few centuries earlier, when England was itself, and had its peculiar manners and customs. As he lives at some distance from the main road, in rather a lonely part of the country, without any rival gentry near him, he has that most enviable of all blessings to an Englishman, an opportunity of indulging the bent of his own humour without molestation. Being representative of the oldest family in the neighbourhood, and a great part of the peasantry being his tenants, he is much looked up to, and, in general, is known simply by the appellation of 'The Squire;' a title which has been accorded to the head of the family since time immemorial. I think it best to give you these hints about my worthy old father, to prepare you for any little eccentricities that might otherwise appear absurd."

We had passed for some time along the wall

of a park, and at length the chaise stopped at the gate.   It was in a heavy magnificent old style, of iron bars, fancifully wrought at top into flourishes and flowers.   The huge square columns that supported the gate were surmounted by the family crest.   Close adjoining was the porter's lodge, sheltered under dark fir-trees, and almost buried in shrubbery.

The post-boy rang a large porter's bell, which resounded through the still frosty air, and was answered by the distant barking of dogs, with which the mansion-house seemed garrisoned.   An old woman immediately ap-  peared at the gate.   As the moonlight fell strongly upon her, I had a full view of a little primitive dame, dressed very much in the antique taste, with a neat kerchief and stomacher, and her silver hair peeping from under a cap of snowy whiteness.

"It was in a heavy magnificent old style, of iron bars, fancifully wrought at top into flourishes and flowers."—PAGE 46.

She came curtseying forth, with many expressions of simple joy at seeing her young master. Her husband, it seems, was up at the house keeping Christmas eve in the servants' hall; they could not do without him, as he was the best hand at a song and story in the household.

My friend proposed that we should alight and walk through the park to the hall, which was at no great distance, while the chaise should follow on. Our road wound through a noble avenue of trees, among the naked branches of which the moon glittered as she rolled through the deep vault of a cloudless sky. The lawn beyond was sheeted with a slight covering of snow, which here and there sparkled as the moonbeams caught a frosty crystal; and at a distance might be seen a thin transparent vapour, stealing up from the low grounds, and threatening gradually to shroud the landscape.

My companion looked round him with transport :—" How often," said he, "have I scampered

up this avenue, on returning home on school
vacations! How often have I played under these
trees when a boy! I feel a degree of filial
reverence for them, as we look up to those who
have cherished us in childhood. My father was
always scrupulous in exacting our holidays, and
having us around him on family festivals. He
used to direct and superintend our games with the
strictness that some parents do the studies of
their children. He was very particular that we
should play the old English games according to
their original form; and consulted old books for
precedent and authority for every 'merrie disport;'
yet I assure you there never was pedantry so
delightful. It was the policy of the good old
gentleman to make his children feel that home
was the happiest place in the world; and I value
this delicious home-feeling as one of the choicest
gifts a parent can bestow."

We were interrupted by the clangour of a
troop of dogs of all sorts and sizes, "mongrel,

puppy, whelp and hound, and curs of low degree,"
that, disturbed by the ringing of the porter's bell,

and the rattling of the chaise, came bounding,
open-mouthed, across the lawn.

———" The little dogs and all,
Tray, Blanch, and Sweetheart—see they bark at me !"

cried Bracebridge, laughing.   At the sound of his

voice the bark was changed into a yelp of delight, and in a moment he was surrounded and almost overpowered by the caresses of the faithful animals.

We had now come in full view of the old family mansion, partly thrown in deep shadow, and partly lit up by the cold moonshine. It was an irregular building of some magnitude, and seemed to be of the architecture of different periods. One wing was evidently very ancient, with heavy stone-shafted bow windows jutting out and overrun with ivy, from among the foliage of which the small diamond-shaped panes of glass glittered with the moonbeams. The rest of the house was in the French taste of Charles the Second's time, having been repaired and altered, as my friend told me, by one of his ancestors, who returned with that monarch at the Restoration. The grounds about the house were laid out in the old formal manner of artificial flower-beds, clipped shrubberies, raised terraces, and heavy stone balustrades, ornamented with urns, a leaden statue or two, and a jet of water. The old gentleman, I was told, was extremely careful to preserve this obsolete finery in all its original state. He admired this fashion in gardening; it had an air of magnificence, was courtly and noble, and befitting good old family style. The boasted imitation of nature in modern gardening had sprung up with modern republican notions, but did not suit a monarchical government; it smacked of the levelling system.—I could not help smiling at this introduction of politics into gardening, though I expressed some apprehension that I should find the old gentleman rather intolerant in his creed.—Frank assured me, however, that it was almost the only instance in which he had ever heard his father meddle with politics; and he believed that he had got this notion from a member of parliament who once passed a few weeks with him. The Squire was glad of any argument to defend his clipped yew-trees and formal terraces, which had been occasionally attacked by modern landscape-gardeners.

As we approached the house, we heard the sound of music, and now and then a burst of laughter from one end of the building. This, Bracebridge said, must proceed from the servants' hall, where a great deal of revelry was permitted, and even encouraged, by the Squire throughout the twelve days of Christmas, provided everything was done conformably to ancient usage. Here were kept up the old games of hoodman blind, shoe the wild mare, hot cockles, steal the white loaf, bob apple, and snapdragon : the

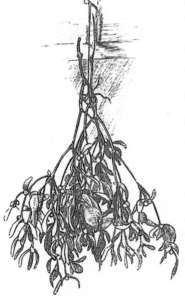

Yule log and Christmas candle were regularly

burnt, and the mistletoe, with its white berries, hung up, to the imminent peril of all the pretty housemaids.*

So intent were the servants upon their sports, that we had to ring repeatedly before we could make ourselves heard. On our arrival being

* See Note A.

announced, the Squire came out to receive us, accompanied by his two other sons; one a young officer in the army, home on leave of absence; the other an Oxonian, just from the university. The Squire was a fine, healthy-looking old gentleman, with silver hair curling lightly round an open florid countenance; in which a physiognomist, with the advantage, like myself, of a previous hint or two, might discover a singular mixture of whim and benevolence.

The family meeting was warm and affectionate; as the evening was far advanced, the Squire would not permit us to change our travelling dresses, but ushered us at once to the company, which was assembled in a large old-fashioned hall. It was composed of different branches of a numerous family connection, where there were the usual proportion of old uncles and aunts, comfortably married dames, superannuated spinsters, blooming country cousins, half-fledged striplings, and bright-eyed boarding-school hoydens.

" The company, which was assembled in a large old-fashioned hall."—PAGE 54.

They were variously occupied; some at a round game of cards; others conversing around the fireplace; at one end of the hall was a group of the young folks, some nearly grown up, others of a more tender and budding age, fully engrossed by

a merry game; and a profusion of wooden horses, penny trumpets, and tattered dolls, about the floor, showed traces of a troop of little fairy beings, who having frolicked through a happy day, had been carried off to slumber through a peaceful night.

While the mutual greetings were going on between Bracebridge and his relatives, I had time to scan the apartment. I have called it a hall, for so it had certainly been in old times, and the Squire had evidently endeavoured to restore it to something of its primitive state. Over the heavy projecting fireplace was suspended a picture of a warrior in armour, standing by a white horse, and on the opposite wall hung helmet, buckler, and lance. At one end an enormous pair of antlers were inserted in the wall, the branches serving as hooks on which to suspend hats, whips, and spurs; and in the corners of the apartment were fowling-pieces, fishing-rods, and other sporting implements. The furniture was of the cumbrous workmanship of former days, though some articles of modern convenience had been added, and the oaken floor had been carpeted; so that the whole presented an odd mixture of parlour and hall.

The grate had been removed from the wide

overwhelming fireplace, to make way for a fire of
wood, in the midst of which was an enormous log

glowing and blazing, and sending forth a vast
volume of light and heat; this I understood was
the Yule-log, which the Squire was particular in

having brought in and illumined on a Christmas eve, according to ancient custom.*

It was really delightful to see the old Squire seated in his hereditary elbow-chair by the

hospitable fireside of his ancestors, and looking around him like the sun of a system, beaming warmth and gladness to every heart. Even the very dog that lay stretched at his feet, as he lazily shifted his position and yawned, would look

* See Note B.

fondly up in his master's face, wag his tail against the floor, and stretch himself again to sleep, confident of kindness and protection. There is an emanation from the heart in genuine hospitality which cannot be described, but is immediately felt, and puts the stranger at once at his ease. I had not been seated many minutes by the comfortable hearth of the worthy cavalier before I found myself as much at home as if I had been one of the family.

Supper was announced shortly after our arrival. It was served up in a spacious oaken chamber, the panels of which shone with wax, and around which were several family portraits decorated with holly and ivy. Beside the accustomed lights, two great wax tapers, called Christmas candles, wreathed with greens, were placed on a highly-polished buffet among the family plate. The table was abundantly spread with substantial fare; but the Squire made his supper of frumenty, a dish made of wheat cakes

boiled in milk with rich spices, being a standing dish in old times for Christmas eve. I was happy to find my old friend, minced-pie, in the retinue of the feast; and finding him to be perfectly orthodox, and that I need not be ashamed of my predilection, I greeted him with all the warmth wherewith we usually greet an old and very genteel acquaintance.

The mirth of the company was greatly promoted by the humours of an eccentric personage whom Mr. Bracebridge always addressed with the quaint appellation of Master Simon. He was a tight, brisk little man, with the air of an arrant old bachelor. His nose was shaped like the bill of a parrot; his face slightly pitted with the small-pox,

with a dry perpetual bloom on it, like a frost-bitten leaf in autumn. He had an eye of great quickness and vivacity, with a drollery and lurking waggery of expression that was irresistible. He was evidently the wit of the family, dealing very much in

sly jokes and innuendoes with the ladies, and making
infinite merriment by harpings upon old themes;
which, unfortunately, my ignorance of the family
chronicles did not permit me to enjoy.   It seemed
to be his great delight during supper to keep a
young girl next him in a continual agony of stifled
laughter, in spite of her awe of the reproving looks

of her mother, who sat opposite.   Indeed, he was
the idol of the younger part of the company, who
laughed at everything he said or did, and at every
turn of his countenance.   I could not wonder at
it; for he must have been a miracle of accom-

plishments in their eyes. He could imitate
Punch and Judy; make an old woman of his
hand, with the assistance of a burnt cork and
pocket-handkerchief; and cut an orange into such
a ludicrous caricature, that the young folks were
ready to die with laughing.

I was let briefly into his history by Frank
Bracebridge. He was an old bachelor of a small
independent income, which by careful manage-
ment was sufficient for all his wants. He revolved
through the family system like a vagrant comet in
its orbit; sometimes visiting one branch, and
sometimes another quite remote; as is often the
case with gentlemen of extensive connections and
small fortunes in England. He had a chirping,
buoyant disposition, always enjoying the present
moment; and his frequent change of scene and
company prevented his acquiring those rusty unac-
commodating habits with which old bachelors are
so uncharitably charged. He was a complete family
chronicle, being versed in the genealogy, history,

and intermarriages of the whole house of Bracebridge, which made him a great favourite with
the old folks ; he was a beau of all the elder ladies
and superannuated spinsters, among whom he
was habitually considered rather a young fellow,
and he was a master of the revels among the
children ; so that there was not a more popular
being in the sphere in which he moved than Mr.
Simon Bracebridge.   Of late years he had
resided almost entirely with the Squire, to whom
he had become a factotum, and whom he particularly delighted by jumping with his humour in
respect to old times, and by having a scrap of
an old song to suit every occasion.   We had
presently a specimen of his last-mentioned talent ;
for no sooner was supper removed, and spiced
wines and other beverages peculiar to the season
introduced, than Master Simon was called on for
a good old Christmas song.   He bethought himself for a moment, and then, with a sparkle of the
eye, and a voice that was by no means bad,

excepting that it ran occasionally into a falsetto, like the notes of a split reed, he quavered forth a quaint old ditty,—

Now Christmas is come,
Let us beat up the drum,
And call all our neighbours together ;
And when they appear,
Let us make them such cheer,
As will keep out the wind and the weather, etc.

The supper had disposed every one to gaiety, and an old harper was summoned from the

F

servants' hall, where he had been strumming all
the evening, and to all appearance comforting
himself with some of the Squire's home-brewed.
He was a kind of hanger-on, I was told, of the
establishment, and though ostensibly a resident
of the village, was oftener to be found in the
Squire's kitchen than his own home, the old
gentleman being fond of the sound of "harp in
hall."

The dance, like most dances after supper, was
a merry one; some of the older folks joined in it,
and the Squire himself figured down several
couples with a partner with whom he affirmed he
had danced at every Christmas for nearly half-a-
century. Master Simon, who seemed to be a
kind of connecting link between the old times and
the new, and to be withal a little antiquated in the
taste of his accomplishments, evidently piqued
himself on his dancing, and was endeavouring to
gain credit by the heel and toe, rigadoon, and
other graces of the ancient school; but he had

unluckily assorted himself with a little romping girl from boarding-school, who, by her wild vivacity, kept him continually on the stretch, and defeated all his sober attempts at elegance ;—such are the ill-assorted matches to which antique gentlemen are unfortunately prone!

The young Oxonian, on the contrary, had led
out one of his maiden aunts, on whom the rogue

played a thousand little knaveries with impunity;
he was full of practical jokes, and his delight was
to tease his aunts and cousins; yet, like all

madcap youngsters, he was a universal favourite among the women. The most interesting couple in the dance was the young officer and a ward of the Squire's, a beautiful blushing girl of seventeen. From several shy glances which I had noticed in the course of the evening, I suspected there was a little kindness growing up between them; and, indeed, the young soldier was just the hero to captivate a romantic girl. He was tall, slender, and handsome, and, like most young British officers of late years, had picked up various small accomplishments on the Continent —he could talk French and Italian—draw landscapes, sing very tolerably—dance divinely; but, above all, he had been wounded at Waterloo:— what girl of seventeen, well read in poetry and romance, could resist such a mirror of chivalry and perfection!

The moment the dance was over, he caught up a guitar, and lolling against the old marble fireplace, in an attitude which I am half inclined to suspect was studied, began the little French air of the Troubadour. The Squire, however,

exclaimed against having anything on Christmas eve but good old English ; upon which the young minstrel, casting up his eye for a moment, as if in an effort of memory, struck into another strain, and, with a charming air of gallantry, gave Herrick's " Night-Piece to Julia :"—

> Her eyes the glow-worm lend thee,
> The shooting stars attend thee,
>   And the elves also,
>   Whose little eyes glow
> Like the sparks of fire, befriend thee.
>
> No Will-o'-the-Wisp mislight thee ;
> Nor snake or glow-worm bite thee ;
>   But on, on thy way,
>   Not making a stay,
> Since ghost there is none to affright thee.
>
> Then let not the dark thee cumber ;
> What though the moon does slumber,
>   The stars of the night
>   Will lend thee their light,
> Like tapers clear without number.
>
> Then, Julia, let me woo thee,
> Thus, thus to come unto me ;
>   And when I shall meet
>   Thy silvery feet,
> My soul I'll pour into thee.

The song might have been intended in compliment to the fair Julia, for so I found his partner was called, or it might not; she, however, was certainly unconscious of any such application, for she never looked at the singer, but kept her eyes cast upon the floor. Her face was suffused, it is true, with a beautiful blush, and there was a gentle heaving of the bosom, but all that was doubtless caused by the exercise of the dance; indeed, so great was her indifference, that she was amusing herself with plucking to pieces a choice bouquet of hothouse flowers, and by the time the song was concluded, the nosegay lay in ruins on the floor.

The party now broke up for the night with the kind-hearted old custom of shaking hands. As I passed through the hall, on the way to my chamber, the dying embers of the *Yule-clog* still sent forth a dusky glow; and had it not been the season when "no spirit dares stir abroad," I should have been half tempted to steal from my room at midnight, and peep whether the fairies might not be at their revels about the hearth.

" Indeed, so great was her indifference, that she was amusing herself with plucking to pieces a
choice bouquet of hot-house flowers."—PAGE 72.

My chamber was in the old part of the mansion, the ponderous furniture of which might have been fabricated in the days of the giants. The room was panelled with cornices of heavy carved-work, in which flowers and grotesque faces were strangely intermingled; and a row of black-looking portraits stared mournfully at me from the walls. The bed was of rich though faded damask, with a lofty tester, and stood in a niche opposite a bow-window. I had scarcely got into bed when a strain of music seemed to break forth in the air just below the window. I listened, and found it proceeded from a band, which I concluded to be the waits from some neighbouring village. They went round the house, playing under the windows. I drew aside the curtains, to hear them more distinctly. The moonbeams fell through the upper part of the casement, partially lighting up the antiquated apartment. The sounds, as they receded, became more soft and aërial, and seemed to accord with quiet and moonlight. I listened and listened—they became more and more tender and remote, and, as they gradually died away, my head sank upon the pillow and I fell asleep.

Christmas Day

Dark and dull night, flie hence away,
And give the honour to this day
That sees December turn'd to May.

*   *   *   *   *

Why does the chilling winter's morne
Smile like a field beset with corn?
Or smell like to a meade new-shorne,
Thus on the sudden?—Come and see
The cause why things thus fragrant be.

HERRICK.

CHRISTMAS DAY

HEN I awoke the next morning, it seemed as if all the events of the preceding evening had been a dream, and nothing but the identity of the ancient chamber convinced me of their reality. While I lay musing on my pillow, I heard the sound of little feet pattering outside of the door, and a whispering consultation.   Presently a choir of small voices

chanted forth an old Christmas carol, the burden of which was,

> Rejoice, our Saviour he was born
> On Christmas Day in the morning.

I rose softly, slipped on my clothes, opened the

door suddenly, and beheld one of the most beautiful little fairy groups that a painter could imagine. It consisted of a boy and two girls, the eldest not more than six, and lovely as seraphs. They were going the rounds of the house, and singing at every chamber-door; but my sudden appearance frightened them into mute bashfulness. They remained for a moment playing on their lips with their fingers, and now and then stealing a shy glance, from under their eyebrows, until, as if by one impulse, they scampered away, and as they turned an angle of the gallery, I heard them laughing in triumph at their escape.

Everything conspired to produce kind and happy feelings in this stronghold of old-fashioned hospitality. The window of my chamber looked out upon what in summer would have been a beautiful landscape. There was a sloping lawn, a fine stream winding at the foot of it, and a tract of park beyond, with noble clumps of trees, and herds of deer. At a distance was a neat hamlet,

with the smoke from
the cottage chimneys
hanging over it; and
a church with its dark
spire in strong relief
against the clear cold
sky. The house was
surrounded with ever-
greens, according to
the English custom,
which   would   have
given almost an appearance
of summer; but the morn-
ing was extremely frosty;
the light vapour of the preceding
evening had been precipitated by
the cold, and covered all the
trees and every blade of grass
with its fine crystallisations. The
rays of a bright morning sun had
a dazzling effect among the glitter-

ing foliage. A robin, perched upon the top of a mountain-ash that hung its clusters of red berries just before my window, was basking himself in the sunshine, and piping a few querulous notes ; and a peacock was displaying all the glories of his train, and strutting with the pride and gravity of a Spanish grandee on the terrace-walk below.

I had scarcely dressed myself, when a servant appeared to invite me to family prayers. He showed me the way to a small chapel in the old

wing of the house, where I found the principal part of the family already assembled in a kind of gallery, furnished with cushions, hassocks, and large prayer-books ; the servants were seated on benches below. The old gentleman read prayers from a desk in front of the gallery, and Master Simon acted as clerk,

G

and made the responses; and I must do him the justice to say that he acquitted himself with great gravity and decorum.

The service was followed by a Christmas carol, which Mr. Bracebridge himself had constructed from a poem of his favourite author, Herrick; and it had been adapted to an old church melody by Master Simon. As there were several good voices among the household, the effect was extremely pleasing; but I was particularly gratified by the exaltation of heart, and sudden sally of grateful feeling, with which the worthy Squire delivered one stanza: his eyes glistening, and his voice rambling out of all the bounds of time and tune:

> "'Tis Thou that crown'st my glittering hearth
>   With guiltlesse mirth,
> And giv'st me wassaile bowles to drink,
>   Spiced to the brink:
> Lord, 'tis Thy plenty-dropping hand
>   That soiles my land;
> And giv'st me for my bushell sowne,
>   Twice ten for one."

I afterwards understood that early morning service was read on every Sunday and saint's day throughout the year, either by Mr. Bracebridge or by some member of the family. It was once almost universally the case at the seats of the nobility and gentry of England, and it is much to be regretted that the custom is fallen into neglect; for the dullest observer must be sensible of the order and serenity prevalent in those households, where the occasional exercise of a beautiful form of worship in the morning gives, as it were, the key-note to every temper for the day, and attunes every spirit to harmony.

Our breakfast consisted of what the Squire denominated true old English fare. He indulged in some bitter lamentations over modern breakfasts of tea-and-toast, which he censured as among the causes of modern effeminacy and weak nerves, and the decline of old English heartiness; and though he admitted them to his table to suit the palates of his guests, yet there was a brave

display of cold meats, wine and ale, on the
sideboard.

After breakfast I walked about the grounds
with Frank Bracebridge and Master Simon, or
Mr. Simon, as he was called by everybody but
the Squire. We were escorted by a number of
gentlemen-like dogs, that seemed loungers about
the establishment; from the frisking spaniel to
the steady old stag-hound ; the last of which was

of a race that had been in the family time out of
mind : they were all obedient to a dog-whistle

which hung to Master Simon's button-hole, and
in the midst of their gambols would glance an
eye occasionally upon a small switch he carried
in his hand.

The old mansion had a still more venerable look in the yellow sunshine than by pale moonlight; and I could not but feel the force of the Squire's idea, that the formal terraces, heavily moulded balustrades, and clipped yew-trees, carried with them an air of proud aristocracy. There appeared to be an unusual number of peacocks about the place, and I was making some remarks upon what I termed a flock of them, that were basking under a sunny wall, when I was gently corrected in my phraseology by Master Simon, who told me that, according to the most ancient and approved treatise on hunting, I must say a *muster* of peacocks. "In the same way," added he, with a slight air of pedantry, "we say a flight of doves or swallows, a bevy of quails, a herd of deer, of wrens, or cranes, a skulk of foxes, or a building of rooks." He went on to inform me that, according to Sir Anthony Fitzherbert, we ought to ascribe to this bird "both understanding and glory; for being praised, he will presently set up his tail chiefly against the sun, to the intent you may the better behold the beauty thereof. But at the fall of the leaf, when his tail falleth, he will mourn and hide himself in corners, till his tail come again as it was."

I could not help smiling at this display of small erudition on so whimsical a subject; but I found that the peacocks were birds of some consequence at the hall, for Frank Bracebridge informed me that they were great favourites with his father, who was extremely careful to keep up the breed; partly because they belonged to chivalry, and were in great request at the stately banquets of the olden time; and partly because they had a pomp and magnificence about them, highly becoming an old family mansion. Nothing, he was accustomed to say, had an air of greater state and dignity than a peacock perched upon an antique stone balustrade.

Master Simon had now to hurry off, having an appointment at the parish church with the

village choristers, who were to perform some music
of his selection.   There was something extremely
agreeable in the cheerful flow of animal spirits of
the little man ; and I confess I had been somewhat surprised at his apt quotations from authors
who certainly were not in the range of every-day

reading.   I mentioned this last circumstance to
Frank Bracebridge, who told me with a smile
that Master Simon's whole stock of erudition was
confined to some half-a-dozen old authors, which
the Squire had put into his hands, and which he
read over and over, whenever he had a studious
fit ; as he sometimes had on a rainy day, or a
long winter evening.   Sir Anthony Fitzherbert's
Book of Husbandry ; Markham's Country Contentments ; the Tretyse of Hunting, by Sir
Thomas Cockayne, Knight; Izaak Walton's
Angler, and two or three more such ancient
worthies of the pen, were his standard authorities ;
and, like all men who know but a few books, he
looked up to them with a kind of idolatry, and
quoted them on all occasions.   As to his songs,
they were chiefly picked out of old books in the
Squire's library, and adapted to tunes that were
popular among the choice spirits of the last
century.   His practical application of scraps of
literature, however, had caused him to be looked

upon as a prodigy of book-knowledge by all the grooms, huntsmen, and small sportsmen of the neighbourhood.

While we were talking we heard the distant toll of the village bell, and I was told that the Squire was a little particular in having his household at church on a Christmas morning; considering it a day of pouring out of thanks and rejoicing; for, as old Tusser observed,

"At Christmas be merry, *and thankful withal*,
And feast thy poor neighbours, the great and the small."

"If you are disposed to go to church," said Frank Bracebridge, "I can promise you a specimen of my cousin Simon's musical achievements. As the church is destitute of an organ, he has formed a band from the village amateurs, and established a musical club for their improvement; he has also sorted a choir, as he sorted my father's pack of hounds, according to the directions of Jervaise Markham, in his Country Contentments; for the bass he has sought out all the

'deep, solemn mouths,' and for the tenor the 'loud
ringing mouths,' among the country bumpkins;
and for 'sweet mouths,' he has culled with curious
taste among the prettiest lasses in the neighbourhood; though these last, he affirms, are the most
difficult to keep in tune; your pretty female singer
being exceedingly wayward and capricious, and
very liable to accident."

As the morning, though frosty, was remarkably

fine and clear, the most of the family walked
to the church, which was a very old building of
gray stone, and stood near a village, about half-a-
mile from the park gate. Adjoining it was a low
snug parsonage, which seemed coeval with the
church. The front of it was perfectly matted
with a yew-tree that had been trained against its
walls, through the dense foliage of which aper-
tures had been formed to admit light into the
small antique lattices. As we passed this
sheltered nest, the parson issued forth and pre-
ceded us.

I had expected to see a sleek well-conditioned
pastor, such as is often found in a snug living in
the vicinity of a rich patron's table; but I was
disappointed. The parson was a little, meagre,
black-looking man, with a grizzled wig that was
too wide, and stood off from each ear; so that
his head seemed to have shrunk away within it,
like a dried filbert in its shell. He wore a rusty
coat, with great skirts, and pockets that would

have held the church Bible and prayer-book ; and
his small legs seemed still smaller, from being

planted in large shoes, decorated with enormous
buckles.

I was informed by Frank Bracebridge that
the parson had been a chum of his father's at

Oxford, and had received this living shortly after
the latter had come to his estate.   He was a complete black-letter hunter, and would scarcely read
a work printed in the Roman character.   The
editions of Caxton and Wynkin de Worde were
his delight; and he was indefatigable in his
researches after such old English writers as have
fallen into oblivion from their worthlessness.   In
deference, perhaps, to the notions of Mr. Bracebridge, he had made diligent investigations into
the festive rights and holiday customs of former
times; and had been as zealous in the inquiry, as
if he had been a boon companion ; but it was
merely with that plodding spirit with which men
of adust temperament follow up any track of
study, merely because it is denominated learning ;
indifferent to its intrinsic nature, whether it be the
illustration of the wisdom, or of the ribaldry and
obscenity of antiquity.   He had poured over these
old volumes so intensely, that they seemed to
have been reflected into his countenance indeed ;

"On reaching the church-porch, we found the parson rebuking the gray-headed sexton for having used mistletoe."—PAGE 95.

which, if the face be an index of the mind, might be compared to a title-page of black-letter.

On reaching the church-porch, we found the parson rebuking the gray-headed sexton for having used mistletoe among the greens with which the church was decorated. It was, he observed, an unholy plant, profaned by having been used by the Druids in their mystic cere-monies; and though it might be innocently employed in the festive ornamenting of halls and kitchens, yet it had been deemed by the Fathers of the Church as unhallowed, and totally unfit for sacred purposes. So tenacious was he on this point, that the poor sexton was obliged to strip down a great part of the humble trophies of his taste, before the parson would consent to enter upon the service of the day.

The interior of the church was venerable but simple; on the walls were several mural monu-ments of the Bracebridges, and just beside the altar was a tomb of ancient workmanship, on which lay the effigy of a warrior in armour, with his legs crossed, a sign of his having been a crusader. I was told it was one of the family who had signalised himself in the Holy Land, and the same whose picture hung over the fireplace in the hall.

During service, Master Simon stood up in the pew, and repeated the responses very audibly; evincing that kind of ceremonious devotion punctually observed by a gentleman of the old school, and a man of old family connections. I observed, too, that he turned over the leaves of a folio prayer-book with something of a flourish; possibly to show off an enormous seal-ring which

"The orchestra was in a small gallery, and presented a most whimsical grouping of heads."—

PAGE 97.

enriched one of his fingers, and which had the
look of a family relic.   But he was evidently most
solicitous about the musical part of the service,
keeping his eye fixed intently on the choir,
and beating time with much gesticulation and
emphasis.

The orchestra was in a small gallery, and
presented a most whimsical grouping of heads,

H

piled one above the other, among which I particularly noticed that of the village tailor, a pale
fellow with a retreating forehead and chin, who

played on the clarionet, and seemed to have blown
his face to a point; and there was another, a
short pursy man, stooping and labouring at a bass
viol, so as to show nothing but the top of a round
bald head, like the egg of an ostrich. There
were two or three pretty faces among the female

singers, to which the keen air of a frosty morning had given a bright rosy tint; but the gentlemen choristers had evidently been chosen, like old Cremona fiddles, more for tone than looks; and as several had to sing from the same book, there were clusterings of odd physiognomies, not unlike those groups of cherubs we sometimes see on country tombstones.

The usual services of the choir were managed tolerably well, the vocal parts generally lagging a little behind the instrumental, and some loitering fiddler now and then making up for lost time by travelling over a passage with prodigious celerity, and clearing more bars than the keenest fox-hunter, to be in at the death. But the great trial was an anthem that had been prepared and arranged by Master Simon, and on which he had founded great expectation. Unluckily there was a blunder at the very outset; the musicians became flurried; Master Simon was in a fever, everything went on lamely and irregularly until they came to a chorus beginning "Now let us sing with one accord," which seemed to be a signal for parting company: all became discord and confusion; each shifted for himself, and got to the end as well, or rather as soon, as he could, excepting one old chorister in a pair of horn spec-

tacles bestriding and pinching a long sonorous nose; who, happening to stand a little apart, and being wrapped up in his own melody, kept on a quavering course, wriggling his head, ogling his book, and winding all up by a nasal solo of at least three bars' duration.

The parson gave us a most erudite sermon on the rites and ceremonies of Christmas, and the propriety of observing it not merely as a day of thanksgiving, but of rejoicing; supporting the correctness of his opinions by the earliest usages of the Church, and enforcing them by the authorities of Theophilus of Cesarea, St. Cyprian, St. Chrysostom, St. Augustine, and a cloud more of Saints and Fathers, from whom he made copious quotations. I was a little at a loss to perceive the necessity of such a mighty array of forces to maintain a point which no one present seemed inclined to dispute; but I soon found that the good man had a legion of ideal adversaries to contend with; having in the course of his researches on the subject of Christmas, got completely embroiled in the sectarian controversies of the Revolution, when the Puritans made such a fierce assault upon the ceremonies of the Church, and poor old Christmas was driven out of the land by proclamation of parliament.* The worthy parson lived but with times past, and knew but a little of the present.

* See Note C.

Shut up among worm-eaten tomes in the retirement of his antiquated little study, the pages of old times were to him as the gazettes of the day; while the era of the Revolution was mere modern history. He forgot that nearly two centuries had elapsed since the fiery persecution of poor mince-pie throughout the land; when plum-porridge was denounced as "mere popery," and roast beef as antichristian; and that Christmas had been brought in again triumphantly with the merry court of King Charles at the Restoration. He kindled into warmth with the ardour of his contest, and the host of imaginary foes with whom he had to combat; had a stubborn conflict with old Prynne and two or three other forgotten champions of the Roundheads, on the subject of Christmas festivity; and concluded by urging his hearers, in the most solemn and affecting manner, to stand to the traditionary customs of their fathers, and feast and make merry on this joyful anniversary of the Church.

I have seldom known a sermon attended apparently with more immediate effects; for on
leaving the church the congregation seemed one
and all possessed with the gaiety of spirit so
earnestly enjoined by their pastor.   The elder folks

gathered in knots in the churchyard, greeting
and shaking hands; and the children ran about
crying, Ule! Ule! and repeating some uncouth

rhymes,* which the parson, who had joined us, informed me had been handed down from days of yore. The villagers doffed their hats to the Squire as he passed, giving him the good wishes of the season with every appearance of heartfelt sincerity, and were invited by him to the hall, to take something to keep out the cold of the weather; and I heard blessings uttered by several of the poor, which convinced me that, in the midst of his enjoyments, the worthy old cavalier had not forgotten the true Christmas virtue of charity.

On our way homeward his heart seemed overflowing with generous and happy feelings. As we passed over a rising ground which commanded something of a prospect, the sounds of rustic merriment now and then reached our ears; the Squire paused for a few moments, and looked around with an air of inexpressible benignity. The beauty of the day was of itself sufficient to

* "Ule! Ule!
Three puddings in a pule;
Crack nuts and cry ule!"

inspire philanthropy.   Notwithstanding the frosti-
ness of the morning, the sun in his cloudless
journey had acquired sufficient power to melt
away the thin covering of snow from every
southern declivity, and to bring out the living
green which adorns an English landscape even in
mid-winter.   Large tracts of smiling verdure con-
trasted with the dazzling whiteness of the shaded
slopes and hollows.   Every sheltered bank, on

which the broad rays rested, yielded its silver rill of cold and limpid water, glittering through the dripping grass; and sent up slight exhalations to contribute to the thin haze that hung just above the surface of the earth. There was something truly cheering in this triumph of warmth and verdure over the frosty thraldom of winter; it was, as the Squire observed, an emblem of Christmas hospitality, breaking through the chills of ceremony and selfishness, and thawing every heart into a flow. He pointed with pleasure to the indications of good cheer reeking from the chimneys of the comfortable farm-houses and low thatched cottages. " I love," said he, "to see this day well kept by rich and poor; it is a great thing to have one day in the year, at least, when you are sure of being welcome wherever you go, and of having, as it were, the world all thrown open to you; and I am almost disposed to join with Poor Robin, in his malediction of every churlish enemy to this honest festival :—

"Those who at Christmas do repine,
    And would fain hence despatch him,
May they with old Duke Humphry dine,
    Or else may Squire Ketch catch 'em."

The Squire went on to lament the deplorable decay of the games and amusements which were once prevalent at this season among the lower orders, and countenanced by the higher : when the old halls of castles and manor-houses were thrown open at daylight ; when the tables were covered with brawn, and beef, and humming ale ; when the harp and the carol resounded all day long, and when rich and poor were alike welcome to enter and make merry.* "Our old games and local customs," said he, "had a great effect in making the peasant fond of his home, and the promotion of them by the gentry made him fond of his lord. They made the times merrier, and kinder, and better ; and I can truly say, with one of our old poets,—

* See Note D.

"I like them well—the curious preciseness
    And all-pretended gravity of those
  That seek to banish hence these harmless sports,
    Have thrust away much ancient honesty.

"The nation," continued he, "is altered; we have almost lost our simple true-hearted peasantry. They have broken asunder from the higher classes, and seem to think their interests

are separate. They have become too knowing, and begin to read newspapers, listen to alehouse politicians, and talk of reform. I think one mode to keep them in good humour in these hard times

would be for the nobility and gentry to pass
more time on their estates, mingle more among
the country people, and set the merry old English
games going again."

Such was the good Squire's project for miti-
gating public discontent; and, indeed, he had
once attempted to put his doctrine in practice,
and a few years before had kept open house
during the holidays in the old style. The country people, however, did not understand how to
play their parts in the scene of hospitality; many
uncouth circumstances occurred; the manor was
overrun by all the vagrants of the country, and
more beggars drawn into the neighbourhood in
one week than the parish officers could get rid of
in a year. Since then he had contented himself
with inviting the decent part of the neighbouring
peasantry to call at the hall on Christmas day,
and distributing beef, and bread, and ale, among
the poor, that they might make merry in their
own dwellings.

We had not been long home when the sound
of music was heard from a distance. A band of
country lads without coats, their shirt-sleeves
fancifully tied with ribands, their hats decorated
with greens, and clubs in their hands, were seen
advancing up the avenue, followed by a large
number of villagers and peasantry. They stopped
before the hall door, where the music struck up
a peculiar air, and the lads performed a curious
and intricate dance, advancing, retreating, and
striking their clubs together, keeping exact time

to the music; while one, whimsically crowned with a fox's skin, the tail of which flaunted down his back, kept capering round the skirts of the dance, and rattling a Christmas-box with many antic gesticulations.

The Squire eyed this fanciful exhibition with great interest and delight, and gave me a full account of its origin, which he traced to the times when the Romans held possession of the island; plainly proving that this was a lineal descendant of the sword-dance of the ancients. "It was now," he said, "nearly extinct, but he had

accidentally met with traces of it in the neighbourhood, and had encouraged its revival; though,
to tell the truth, it was too apt to be followed
up by rough cudgel-play and broken heads in the
evening."

After the dance was concluded, the whole
party was entertained with brawn and beef, and
stout home-brewed. The Squire himself mingled
among the rustics, and was received with awk-
ward demonstrations of deference and regard. It

is true I perceived two or three of the younger
peasants, as they were raising their tankards to

their mouths when the Squire's back was turned, making something of a grimace, and giving each other the wink ; but the moment they caught my eye they pulled grave faces, and were exceedingly demure. With Master Simon, however, they all seemed more at their ease. His varied occupations and amusements had made him well known throughout the neighbourhood. He was a visitor at every farm-house and cottage ; gossiped with the farmers and their wives ; romped with their daughters ; and, like that type of a vagrant bachelor, the humble bee, tolled the sweets from all the rosy lips of the country round.

The bashfulness of the guests soon gave way before good cheer and affability. There is something genuine and affectionate in the gaiety of the lower orders, when it is excited by the bounty and familiarity of those above them ; the warm glow of gratitude enters into their mirth, and a kind word or a small pleasantry, frankly uttered by a patron, gladdens the heart of the dependant more than oil and wine. When the Squire had retired the merriment increased, and there was much joking and laughter, particularly between Master Simon and a hale, ruddy - faced, white - headed farmer, who appeared to be the wit of the village; for I observed all his companions to wait with  open mouths for his retorts, and burst into a gratuitous laugh before they could well understand them.

The whole house indeed seemed abandoned to merriment. As I passed to my room to dress for dinner, I heard the sound of music in a small court, and, looking through a window that commanded it, I perceived a band of wandering musicians, with pandean pipes and tambourine; a pretty coquettish housemaid was dancing a jig with a smart country lad, while several of the other servants were looking on.   In the midst of her sport the girl caught a glimpse of my face at the window, and, colouring up, ran off with an air of roguish affected confusion.

The Christmas Dinner

Lo, now is come the joyful'st feast !
  Let every man be jolly,
Eache roome with yvie leaves is drest,
  And every post with holly.
Now all our neighbours' chimneys smoke,
  And Christmas blocks are burning ;
Their ovens they with bak't meats choke,
  And all their spits are turning.
    Without the door let sorrow lie,
      And if, for cold, it hap to die,
    We'll bury't in a Christmas pye,
      And evermore be merry.
                    WITHERS'S *Juvenilia.*

THE CHRISTMAS DINNER

I HAD finished my
toilet, and was loiter-
ing with Frank Brace-
bridge in the library, when
we heard a distant
thwacking sound,
which he informed me was a
signal for the serving up of the dinner. The

Squire kept up old customs in kitchen as well as hall; and the rolling-pin, struck upon the dresser by the cook, summoned the servants to carry in the meats.

> Just in this nick the cook knock'd thrice,
> And all the waiters in a trice
>   His summons did obey;
> Each serving man, with dish in hand,
> March'd boldly up, like our train-band,
>   Presented and away.*

* Sir John Suckling.

The dinner was served up in the great hall, where the Squire always held his Christmas banquet. A blazing crackling fire of logs had been heaped on to warm the spacious apartment, and the flame went sparkling and wreathing up the wide-mouthed chimney. The great picture of the crusader and his white horse had been profusely decorated with greens for the occasion ; and holly and ivy had likewise been wreathed round the helmet and weapons on the opposite wall, which I understood were the arms of the same warrior. I must own, by the by, I had strong doubts about the authenticity of the painting and armour as having belonged to the crusader, they certainly having the stamp of

more recent days ; but I was told that the painting had been so considered time out of mind ;
and that as to the armour, it had been found in
a lumber room, and elevated to its present situa-
tion by the Squire, who at once determined it to
be the armour of the family hero ; and as he was
absolute authority on all such subjects in his own
household, the matter had passed into current

acceptation.   A sideboard was set out just under
this chivalric trophy, on which was a display of

" Never did Christmas board display a more goodly and gracious assemblage of countenances."—
PAGE 123.

plate that might have vied (at least in variety) with Belshazzar's parade of the vessels of the temple; "flagons, cans, cups, beakers, goblets, basins, and ewers;" the gorgeous utensils of good companionship, that had gradually accumulated through many generations of jovial housekeepers. Before these stood the two Yule candles beaming like two stars of the first magnitude; other lights were distributed in branches, and the whole array glittered like a firmament of silver.

We were ushered into this banqueting scene with the sound of minstrelsy, the old harper being seated on a stool beside the fireplace, and twanging his instrument with a vast deal more power than melody. Never did Christmas board display a more goodly and gracious assemblage of countenances: those who were not handsome were, at least, happy; and happiness is a rare improver of your hard-favoured visage. I always consider an old English family as well worth studying as a collection of Holbein's portraits or Albert Durer's

prints. There is much antiquarian lore to be
acquired; much knowledge of the physiognomies
of former times. Perhaps it may be from having
continually before their eyes those rows of old
family portraits, with which the mansions of this
country are stocked; certain it is, that the quaint
features of antiquity are often most faithfully
perpetuated in these ancient lines; and I have
traced an old family nose through a whole picture
gallery, legitimately handed down from generation to generation, almost from the time of the
Conquest. Something of the kind was to be

observed in the worthy company around me. Many of
their faces had evidently
originated in a Gothic age,
and been merely copied by
succeeding generations; and
there was one little girl, in
particular, of staid demean-
our, with a high Roman nose,

and an antique vinegar aspect, who was a great favourite of the Squire's, being, as he said, a Bracebridge all over, and the very counterpart of one of his ancestors who figured in the court of Henry VIII.

The parson said grace, which was not a short familiar one, such as is commonly addressed to the Deity, in these unceremonious days; but a long, courtly, well-worded one of the ancient

school.   There was now a pause, as if something
was expected ; when suddenly the butler entered

the hall with some degree of bustle : he was
attended by a servant on each side with a large
wax-light, and bore a silver dish, on which was an

enormous pig's head decorated with rosemary, with a lemon in its mouth, which was placed with great formality at the head of the table. The moment this pageant made its appearance, the harper struck up a flourish; at the conclusion of which the young Oxonian, on receiving a hint from the Squire, gave, with an air of the most comic gravity, an old carol, the first verse of which was as follows :—

> Caput apri defero
> Reddens laudes Domino.
> The boar's head in hand bring I,
> With garlands gay and rosemary.
> I pray you all synge merily
> Qui estis in convivio.

Though prepared to witness many of these little eccentricities, from being apprised of the peculiar hobby of mine host; yet, I confess, the parade with which so odd a dish was introduced somewhat perplexed me, until I gathered from the conversation of the Squire and the parson that it was meant to represent the bringing in of the

boar's head : a dish formerly served up with much
ceremony, and the sound of minstrelsy and song,
at great tables on Christmas day. " I like the
old custom," said the Squire, " not merely because
it is stately and pleasing in itself, but because it
was observed at the College of Oxford, at which
I was educated. When I hear the old song
chanted, it brings to mind the time when I was
young and gamesome—and the noble old college-
hall—and my fellow-students loitering about in
their black gowns ; many of whom, poor lads, are
now in their graves !"

The parson, however, whose mind was not
haunted by such associations, and who was
always more taken up with the text than the
sentiment, objected to the Oxonian's version
of the carol ; which he affirmed was different
from that sung at college. He went on, with
the dry perseverance of a commentator, to give
the college reading, accompanied by sundry
annotations : addressing himself at first to the

company at large; but finding their attention gradually diverted to other talk, and other objects, he lowered his tone as his number of auditors diminished, until he concluded his remarks, in an under voice, to a fat-headed old gentleman next him, who was silently engaged in the discussion of a huge plateful of turkey.*

The table was literally loaded with good cheer, and presented an epitome of country abundance, in this season of overflowing larders.

* See Note E.

K

A distinguished post was allotted to "ancient sirloin," as mine host termed it; being, as he added, "the standard of old English hospitality, and a joint of goodly presence, and full of expectation." There were several dishes quaintly decorated, and which had evidently something traditionary in their embellishments; but about which, as I did not like to appear over-curious, I asked no questions.

I could not, however, but notice a pie, magnificently decorated with peacocks' feathers, in imitation of the tail of that bird, which overshadowed a considerable tract of the table. This the Squire confessed, with some little hesitation, was a pheasant-pie, though a peacock-pie was certainly the most authentical; but there had been such a mortality among the peacocks this season, that he could not prevail upon himself to have one killed.*

It would be tedious, perhaps, to my wiser readers, who may not have that foolish fondness for odd and obsolete things to which I am a little given, were I to mention the other makeshifts of this worthy old humorist, by which he was endeavouring to follow up, though at humble distance, the quaint customs of antiquity. I was pleased, however, to see the respect shown to his whims by his children and relatives; who, indeed, entered readily into the full spirit of them, and seemed all well versed in their parts; having doubtless been present at many a rehearsal. I was amused, too, at the air of profound gravity

* See Note F.

with which the butler and other servants executed
the duties assigned them, however eccentric.
They had an old-fashioned look ; having, for the
most part, been brought up in the household, and
grown into keeping with the antiquated mansion,
and the humours of its lord ; and most probably
looked upon all his whimsical regulations as the
established laws of honourable housekeeping.

When the cloth was removed, the butler

brought in a huge silver vessel of rare and
curious workmanship, which he placed before the
Squire. Its appearance was hailed with accla-
mation; being the Wassail Bowl, so renowned in
Christmas festivity. The contents had been prepared by the Squire himself; for it was a beverage in the skilful mixture of which he particularly
prided himself; alleging that it was too abstruse
and complex for the comprehension of an ordinary
servant. It was a potation, indeed, that might
well make the heart of a toper leap within him;
being composed of the richest and raciest wines,
highly spiced and sweetened, with roasted apples
bobbing about the surface.*

The old gentleman's whole countenance beamed
with a serene look of indwelling delight, as he
stirred this mighty bowl. Having raised it to his
lips, with a hearty wish of a merry Christmas to
all present, he sent it brimming round the board,
for every one to follow his example, according to

* See Note G.

the primitive style; pronouncing it "the ancient fountain of good feeling, where all hearts met together."*

There was much laughing and rallying as the honest emblem of Christmas joviality circulated, and was kissed rather coyly by the ladies.   When

* See Note H.

it reached Master Simon he raised it in both
hands, and with the air of a boon companion
struck up an old Wassail chanson :

> The browne bowle,
> The merry browne bowle,
> As it goes round about-a,
>> Fill
>> Still,
> Let the world say what it will,
> And drink your fill all out-a.
>
> The deep canne,
> The merry deep canne,
> As thou dost freely quaff-a,
>> Sing,
>> Fling,
> Be as merry as a king,
> And sound a lusty laugh-a.*

Much of the conversation during dinner
turned upon family topics, to which I was a
stranger. There was, however, a great deal of
rallying of Master Simon about some gay widow,
with whom he was accused of having a flirtation.
This attack was commenced by the ladies ; but it

* From " Poor Robin's Almanack."

was continued throughout the dinner by the fat-headed old gentleman next the parson, with the

 persevering assiduity of a slow-hound ; being one of those long-winded jokers, who, though rather dull at starting game, are unrivalled for their talents in hunting it down.   At every pause in the general conversation, he renewed his bantering in pretty much the same terms ; winking hard at me with both eyes whenever he gave Master Simon what he considered a home thrust.   The latter, indeed, seemed fond of being teased on the subject, as old bachelors are apt to be ; and he took occasion to inform me, in an under-tone, that the lady in question was a prodigiously fine woman, and drove her own curricle.

The dinner-time passed away in this flow of innocent hilarity ; and, though the old hall may

have resounded in its time with many a scene of broader rout and revel, yet I doubt whether it ever witnessed more honest and genuine enjoyment. How easy it is for one benevolent being to diffuse pleasure around him; and how truly is a kind heart a fountain of gladness, making everything in its vicinity to freshen into smiles! the joyous disposition of the worthy Squire was perfectly contagious; he was happy himself, and disposed to make all the world happy; and the little eccentricities of his humour did but season, in a manner, the sweetness of his philanthropy.

When the ladies had retired, the conversation, as usual, became still more animated; many good things were broached which had been thought of during dinner, but which would not exactly do for a lady's ear; and though I cannot positively affirm that there was much wit uttered, yet I have certainly heard many contests of rare wit produce much less laughter. Wit, after all, is a mighty tart, pungent ingredient, and much too acid for some stomachs ; but honest good humour is the oil and wine of a merry meeting, and there is no jovial companionship equal to that where the jokes are rather small, and the laughter abundant.

The Squire told several long stories of early college pranks and adventures, in some of which the parson had been a sharer ; though in looking at the latter, it required some effort of imagination to figure such a little dark anatomy of a man into the perpetrator of a madcap gambol.   Indeed, the two college chums presented pictures of what men may be made by their different lots in life.   The Squire had left the university to live lustily on his paternal domains, in the vigorous enjoyment of

prosperity and sunshine, and had flourished on to
a hearty and florid old age; whilst the poor
parson, on the contrary, had dried and withered
away, among dusty tomes, in the silence and
shadows of his study.   Still there seemed to be a
spark of almost extinguished fire, feebly glim-
mering in the bottom of
his soul ; and as the Squire
hinted at a sly story of
the parson and a pretty
milkmaid, whom
they once met
on the banks of
the Isis, the old
gentleman made
an "alphabet of
faces," which, as
far as I could de-
cipher his physi-
ognomy, I verily
believe was in-

dicative of laughter ;—indeed, I have rarely met with an old gentleman who took absolutely offence at the imputed gallantries of his youth.

I found the tide of wine and wassail fast gaining on the dry land of sober judgment. The company grew merrier and louder as their jokes grew duller. Master Simon was in as chirping a

humour as a grasshopper filled with dew; his old songs grew of a warmer complexion, and he began to talk maudlin about the widow. He even gave a long song about the wooing of a widow, which he informed me he had gathered from an excellent black-letter work, entitled "Cupid's Solicitor for Love," containing store of good advice for bachelors, and which he promised to lend me.   The first verse was to this effect :—

> He that will woo a widow must not dally,
> He must make hay while the sun doth shine ;
> He must not stand with her, Shall I, Shall I ?
> But boldly say, Widow, thou must be mine.

This song inspired the fat-headed old gentleman, who made several attempts to tell a rather broad story out of Joe Miller, that was pat to the purpose ; but he always stuck in the middle, everybody recollecting the latter part excepting himself. The parson, too, began to show the effects of good cheer, having gradually settled down into a doze, and his wig sitting most suspiciously on one side. Just at this juncture we were summoned to the drawing-room, and, I suspect, at the private instigation of mine host, whose joviality seemed always tempered with a proper love of decorum.

After the dinner-table was removed, the hall was given up to the younger members of the family, who, prompted to all kind of noisy mirth by the Oxonian and Master Simon, made its old walls ring with their merriment, as they played at romping games. I delight in witnessing the gambols of children, and particularly at this happy holiday-season, and could not help stealing out of the drawing-room on hearing one of their peals of laughter. I found them at the game of blind-man's buff. Master Simon, who was the leader of their revels, and seemed on all occasions to fulfil the office of that ancient potentate, the Lord of Misrule,* was blinded in the midst of the hall. The little beings were as busy about him as the mock fairies about Falstaff; pinching him, pluck-ing at the skirts of his coat, and tickling him with straws. One fine blue-eyed girl of about thirteen, with her flaxen hair all in beautiful confusion, her frolic face in a glow, her frock

* See Note I.

half torn off her shoulders, a complete picture
of a romp, was the chief tormentor; and from
the slyness with which Master Simon avoided
the smaller game, and hemmed this wild little
nymph in corners, and obliged her to jump
shrieking over chairs, I suspected the rogue

of being not a whit more blinded than was convenient.

When I returned to the drawing-room, I found the company seated round the fire, listen-

ing to the parson, who was deeply ensconced in a high-backed oaken chair, the work of some cunning artificer of yore, which had been brought from the library for his particular accommodation. From this venerable piece of furniture, with which his shadowy figure and dark weazen face

so admirably accorded, he was dealing forth
strange accounts of the popular superstitions
and legends of the surrounding country, with
which he had become acquainted in the course
of his antiquarian researches. I am half inclined
to think that the old gentleman was himself
somewhat tinctured with superstition, as men are
very apt to be who live a recluse and studious
life in a sequestered part of the country, and
pore over black-letter tracts, so often filled with
the marvellous and supernatural. He gave us
several anecdotes of the fancies of the neighbouring peasantry, concerning the effigy of the
crusader which lay on the tomb by the church
altar. As it was the only monument of the kind
in that part of the country, it had always been
regarded with feelings of superstition by the
goodwives of the village. It was said to get
up from the tomb and walk the rounds of the
churchyard in stormy nights, particularly when it
thundered; and one old woman, whose cottage

bordered on the churchyard, had seen it, through the windows of the church, when the moon shone, slowly pacing up and down the aisles. It was the belief that some wrong had been left unre- dressed by the deceased, or some treasure hidden, which kept the spirit in a state of trouble and restlessness. Some talked of gold and jewels

buried in the tomb, over which the spectre kept
watch ; and there was a story current of a sexton
in old times who endeavoured to break his way
to the coffin at night ; but just as he reached it,
received a violent blow from the marble hand
of the effigy, which stretched him senseless on
the pavement. These tales were often laughed
at by some of the sturdier among the rustics,
yet when night came on, there were many of the
stoutest unbelievers that were shy of venturing
alone in the footpath that led across the churchyard.

From these and other anecdotes that followed,
the crusader appeared to be the favourite hero
of ghost stories throughout the vicinity. His
picture, which hung up in the hall, was thought
by the servants to have something supernatural
about it ; for they remarked that, in whatever
part of the hall you went, the eyes of the warrior
were still fixed on you. The old porter's wife,
too, at the lodge, who had been born and brought

up in the family, and was a great gossip among
the maid-servants, affirmed, that in her young
days she had often heard say, that on Midsummer
eve, when it is well known all kinds of ghosts,
goblins, and fairies become visible and walk
abroad, the crusader used to mount his horse,

come down from his picture, ride about the house,
down the avenue, and so to the church to visit
the tomb; on which occasion the church-door
most civilly swung open of itself: not that he
needed it; for he rode through closed gates and
even stone walls, and had been seen by one of
the dairymaids to pass between two bars of the
great park gate, making himself as thin as a
sheet of paper.

All these superstitions I found had been very
much countenanced by the Squire, who, though
not superstitious himself, was very fond of seeing
others so.   He listened to every goblin tale of
the neighbouring gossips with infinite gravity,
and held the porter's wife in high favour on
account of her talent for the marvellous.   He
was himself a great reader of old legends and
romances, and often lamented that he could not
believe in them; for a superstitious person, he
thought, must live in a kind of fairyland.

Whilst we were all attention to the parson's

stories, our ears were suddenly assailed by a burst of heterogeneous sounds from the hall, in which was mingled something like the clang of rude minstrelsy, with the uproar of many small voices and girlish laughter. The door suddenly flew open, and a train came trooping into the room, that might almost have been mistaken for the breaking up of the court of Fairy. That indefatigable spirit, Master Simon, in the faithful discharge of his duties as lord of misrule, had conceived the idea of a Christmas mummery, or masquing; and having called in to his assistance the Oxonian and the young officer, who were equally ripe for anything that should occasion romping and merriment, they had carried it into instant effect. The old housekeeper had been consulted; the antique clothes-presses and wardrobes rummaged and made to yield up the relics of finery that had not seen the light for several generations; the younger part of the company had been privately convened from the

parlour and hall, and the whole had been be-
dizened out, into
a burlesque imi-
tation of an an-
tique masque.*

Master Simon
led the van, as
'Ancient Christ-
mas," quaintly
apparelled in a
ruff, a short cloak,
which had very
much the aspect
of one of the old
housekeeper's
petticoats, and a
hat that might
have served for
a village steeple,

and must indubitably have figured in the days of

* See Note J.

the Covenanters. From under this his nose curved boldly forth, flushed with a frost-bitten bloom, that seemed the very trophy of a December blast. He was accompanied by the blue-eyed romp, dished up as "Dame Mince-Pie," in the venerable magnificence of faded brocade, long stomacher, peaked hat, and high-heeled shoes. The young officer appeared as Robin Hood, in a sporting dress of Kendal green, and a foraging cap, with a gold tassel. The costume, to be sure, did not bear testi-

" The rest of the train had been metamorphosed in various ways."—PAGE 153.

mony to deep research, and there was an evident eye to the picturesque, natural to a young gallant in the presence of his mistress. The fair Julia hung on his arm in a pretty rustic dress, as "Maid Marian." The rest of the train had been metamorphosed in various ways ; the girls trussed up in the finery of the ancient belles of the Bracebridge line, and the striplings be-whiskered with burnt cork, and gravely clad in broad skirts, hanging sleeves, and full-bottomed wigs, to represent the characters of Roast Beef, Plum Pud-

ding, and other wor-
thies celebrated in an-
cient maskings. The
whole was under the
control of the Oxoni-
an, in the appropriate
character of Misrule ;
and I observed that
he exercised rather
a mischievous sway
with his wand over
the smaller person-
ages of the pageant.

The irruption of
this motley crew, with
beat of drum, accord-
ing to ancient custom,
was the consumma-
tion of uproar and
merriment. Master
Simon covered him-

self with glory by the stateliness with which, as
Ancient Christmas, he walked a minuet with the
peerless, though giggling, Dame Mince-Pie. It
was followed by a dance of all the characters,
which, from its medley of costumes, seemed as
though the old family portraits had skipped down

from their frames to join in
the sport. Different centuries were figuring at cross
hands and right and left ; the
dark ages were cutting pirou-
ettes and rigadoons ; and the
days of Queen Bess jigging
merrily down the middle,
through a line of succeeding
generations.

The worthy Squire con-
templated these fantastic
sports, and this resurrection
of his old wardrobe, with the
simple relish of childish de-

light.   He stood chuckling and rubbing his hands,
and scarcely hearing a word the parson said, notwithstanding that the latter was discoursing most
authentically on the ancient and stately dance at
the Paon, or Peacock, from which he conceived
the minuet to be derived.*   For my part, I was in
a continual excitement, from the varied scenes of
whim and innocent gaiety passing before me.   It
was inspiring to see wild-eyed frolic and warm-
hearted hospitality breaking out from among
the chills and glooms of winter, and old age
throwing off his apathy, and catching once more
the freshness of youthful enjoyment.   I felt also
an interest in the scene, from the consideration
that these fleeting customs were posting fast into
oblivion, and that this was, perhaps, the only
family in England in which the whole of them
were still punctiliously observed.   There was a
quaintness, too, mingled with all this revelry,
that gave it a peculiar zest ; it was suited to

* See Note K.

the time and place; and as the old Manor House almost reeled with mirth and wassail, it seemed echoing back the joviality of long-departed years.

But enough of Christmas and its gambols; it is time for me to pause in this garrulity. Me-

thinks I hear the questions asked by my graver
readers, "To what purpose is all this?—how is
the world to be made wiser by this talk?"   Alas!
is there not wisdom enough extant for the in-
struction of the world?   And if not, are there
not thousands of abler pens labouring for its
improvement?—It is so much pleasanter to please
than to instruct—to play the companion rather
than the preceptor.

What, after all, is the mite of wisdom that I
could throw into the mass of knowledge? or how
am I sure that my sagest deductions may be safe
guides for the opinions of others?   But in writing
to amuse, if I fail, the only evil is my own dis-
appointment.   If, however, I can by any lucky
chance, in these days of evil, rub out one wrinkle
from the brow of care, or beguile the heavy
heart of one moment of sorrow; if I can now
and then penetrate through the gathering film
of misanthropy, prompt a benevolent view of
human nature, and make my reader more in

good humour with his fellow-beings and himself, surely, surely, I shall not then have written entirely in vain.

NOTES

NOTE A, p. 53.

THE mistletoe is still hung up in farm-houses and kitchens at
Christmas ; and the young men have the privilege of kissing the
girls under it, plucking each time a berry from the bush. When
the berries are all plucked, the privilege ceases.

NOTE B, p. 58.

The *Yule-clog* is a great log of wood, sometimes the root of a
tree, brought into the house with great ceremony, on Christmas
eve, laid in the fireplace, and lighted with the brand of last year's
clog. While it lasted there was great drinking, singing, and telling
of tales. Sometimes it was accompanied by Christmas candles,
but in the cottages the only light was from the ruddy blaze of the
great wood fire. The *Yule-clog* was to burn all night ; if it went
out, it was considered a sign of ill luck.

Herrick mentions it in one of his songs :—

> "Come, bring with a noise
> My merrie, merrie boyes,
> The Christmas log to the firing :
> While my good dame, she
> Bids ye all be free,
> And drink to your hearts' desiring."

The *Yule-clog* is still burnt in many farm-houses and kitchens

M

in England, particularly in the north, and there are several superstitions connected with it among the peasantry.   If a squinting
person come to the house while it is burning, or a person bare-
footed, it is considered an ill omen.   The brand remaining from
the *Yule-clog* is carefully put away to light the next year's Christmas fire.

NOTE C, p. 102.

From the " Flying Eagle," a small Gazette, published December 24, 1652 :—" The House spent much time this day about the
business of the Navy, for settling the affairs at sea ; and before
they rose, were presented with a terrible remonstrance against
Christmas day, grounded upon divine Scriptures, 2 Cor. v. 16 ;
1 Cor. xv. 14, 17 ; and in honour of the Lord's Day, grounded upon
these Scriptures, John xx. 1 ; Rev. i. 10 ; Psalm cxviii. 24 ; Lev.
xxiii. 7, 11 ; Mark xvi. 8 ; Psalm lxxxiv. 10, in which Christmas is
called Anti-Christ's masse, and those Mass-mongers and Papists
who observe it, etc.   In consequence of which Parliament spent
some time in consultation about the abolition of Christmas day,
passed orders to that effect, and resolved to sit on the following
day, which was commonly called Christmas day."

NOTE D, p. 108.

" An English gentleman at the opening of the great day, *i.e.* on
Christmas day in the morning, had all his tenants and neighbours
enter his hall by daybreak.   The strong beer was broached, and
the black jacks went plentifully about with toast, sugar, nutmeg,
and good Cheshire cheese.   The hackin (the great sausage) must

be boiled by daybreak, or else two young men must take the maiden (*i.e.* the cook) by the arms and run her round the market-place till she is shamed of her laziness."—*Round about our Sea-Coal Fire.*

NOTE E, p. 129.

The old ceremony of serving up the boar's head on Christmas day is still observed in the hall of Queen's College, Oxford. I was favoured by the parson with a copy of the carol as now sung, and as it may be acceptable to such of my readers as are curious in these grave and learned matters, I give it entire.

> "The boar's head in hand bear I,
> Bedeck'd with bays and rosemary;
> And I pray you, my masters, be merry,
>   Quot estis in convivio.
>   Caput apri defero
>   Reddens laudes Domino.

> The boar's head, as I understand,
> Is the rarest dish in all this land,
> Which thus bedeck'd with a gay garland
>   Let us servire cantico.
>   Caput apri defero, etc.

> Our steward hath provided this
> In honour of the King of Bliss,
> Which on this day to be served is
>   In Reginensi Atrio.
>   Caput apri defero,"
>   Etc. etc. etc.

NOTE F, p. 131.

The peacock was anciently in great demand for stately enter-
tainments.   Sometimes it was made into a pie, at one end of which
the head appeared above the crust in all its plumage, with the beak
richly gilt ; at the other end the tail was displayed.   Such pies
were served up at the solemn banquets of chivalry, when Knights-
errant pledged themselves to undertake any perilous enterprise ;
whence came the ancient oath, used by Justice Shallow, "by cock
and pie."

The peacock was also an important dish for the Christmas
feast ; and Massinger, in his City Madam, gives some idea of the
extravagance with which this, as well as other dishes, was prepared
for the gorgeous revels of the olden times :—

> "Men may talk of country Christmasses,
>   Their thirty pound butter'd eggs, their pies of carps' tongues :
>   Their pheasants drench'd with ambergris ; *the carcases of three fat
>   wethers bruised for gravy, to make sauce for a single peacock!*"

NOTE G, p. 133.

The Wassail Bowl was sometimes composed of ale instead of
wine ; with nutmeg, sugar, toast, ginger, and roasted crabs ; in this
way the nut-brown beverage is still prepared in some old families,
and round the hearths of substantial farmers at Christmas.   It
is also called Lambs' Wool, and is celebrated by Herrick in his
"Twelfth Night :"—

> "Next crowne the bowle full
>   With gentle Lambs' Wool,
> Add sugar, nutmeg, and ginger,
>   With store of ale too ;
>   And thus ye must doe
> To make the Wassaile a swinger."

NOTE H, p. 134.

"The custom of drinking out of the same cup gave place to each having his cup. When the steward came to the doore with the Wassel, he was to cry three times, *Wassel, Wassel, Wassel,* and then the chappel (chaplain) was to answer with a song.— ARCHÆOLOGIA.

NOTE I, p. 142.

"At Christmasse there was in the Kinge's house, wheresoever hee was lodged, a lorde of misrule, or mayster of merry disportes ; and the like had ye in the house of every nobleman of honor, or good worshippe, were he spirituall or temporall.".—STOW.

NOTE J, p. 151.

Maskings or mummeries were favourite sports at Christmas in old times; and the wardrobes at halls and manor-houses were often laid under contribution to furnish dresses and fantastic disguisings. I strongly suspect Master Simon to have taken the idea of his from Ben Jonson's Masque of Christmas.

NOTE K, p. 156.

Sir John Hawkins, speaking of the dance called the Pavon, from pavo, a peacock, says, " It is a grave and majestic dance ; the method of dancing it anciently was by gentlemen dressed with caps and swords, by those of the long robe in their gowns, by the peers in their mantles, and by the ladies in gowns with long trains, the motion whereof, in dancing, resembled that of a peacock."— *History of Music.*